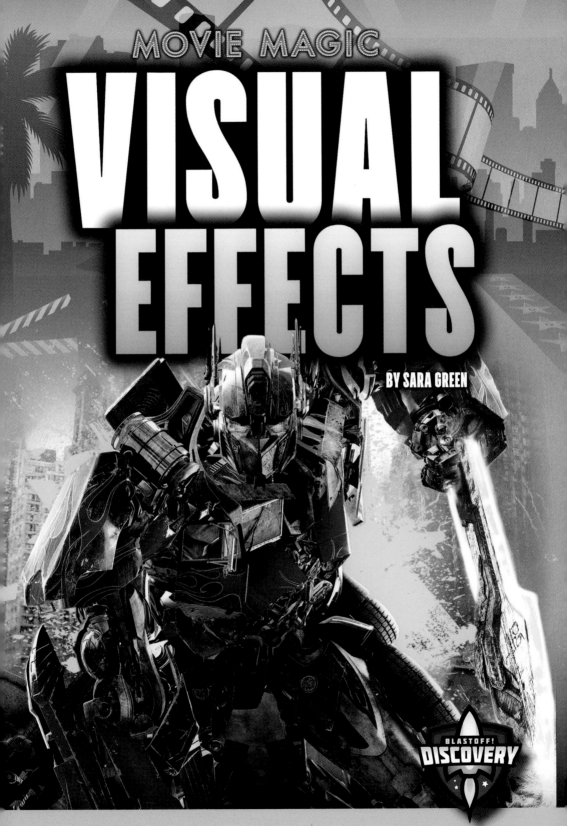

BELLWETHER MEDIA • MINNEAPOLIS, MN

MOVIE MAGIC

VISUAL EFFECTS

BY SARA GREEN

BLASTOFF!
DISCOVERY

Blastoff! Discovery launches
a new mission: reading to learn.
Filled with facts and features, each
book offers you an exciting new
world to explore!

This edition first published in 2020 by Bellwether Media, Inc.

No part of this publication may be reproduced in whole or in
part without written permission of the publisher.
For information regarding permission, write to
Bellwether Media, Inc., Attention: Permissions Department,
6012 Blue Circle Drive, Minnetonka, MN 55343.

Library of Congress Cataloging-in-Publication Data

Names: Green, Sara, 1964- author.
Title: Visual Effects / by Sara Green.
Description: Minneapolis, MN : Bellwether Media, Inc., 2020.
  | Series: Blastoff! Discovery. Movie Magic | Includes
  bibliographical references and index.
Identifiers: LCCN 2019000957 (print) | LCCN 2019001623
  (ebook) | ISBN 9781618915863 (ebook) | ISBN
  9781644870457 (hardcover : alk. paper)
Subjects: LCSH: Cinematography–Special effects–Juvenile
  literature. | Digital cinematography–Juvenile literature. |
  Computer graphics–Juvenile literature.
Classification: LCC TR858 (ebook) | LCC TR858 .G73555
  2020 (print) | DDC 777/.9-dc23
LC record available at https://lccn.loc.gov/2019000957

Editor: Betsy Rathburn   Designer: Brittany McIntosh

Printed in the United States of America, North Mankato, MN.

TABLE OF CONTENTS

OUTER SPACE HEROES!

Rocket Raccoon hides on a tree branch above the ground. He sees his enemies moving through the forest. Suddenly, Rocket begins leaping from branch to branch. He sets off bombs. Explosions light the sky. The enemies cannot escape!

This **scene** is in the 2017 film *Guardians of the Galaxy Vol 2*. On **set**, Rocket was played by an actor. The actor's movements were recorded using **motion capture**. Later, filmmakers used **CGI** to turn the actor into a Raccoon!

ON THE SET OF
*GUARDIANS OF THE GALAXY
VOL. 2*

ROCKET RACCOON

NICKNAME

The term "visual effects" is often shortened to VFX.

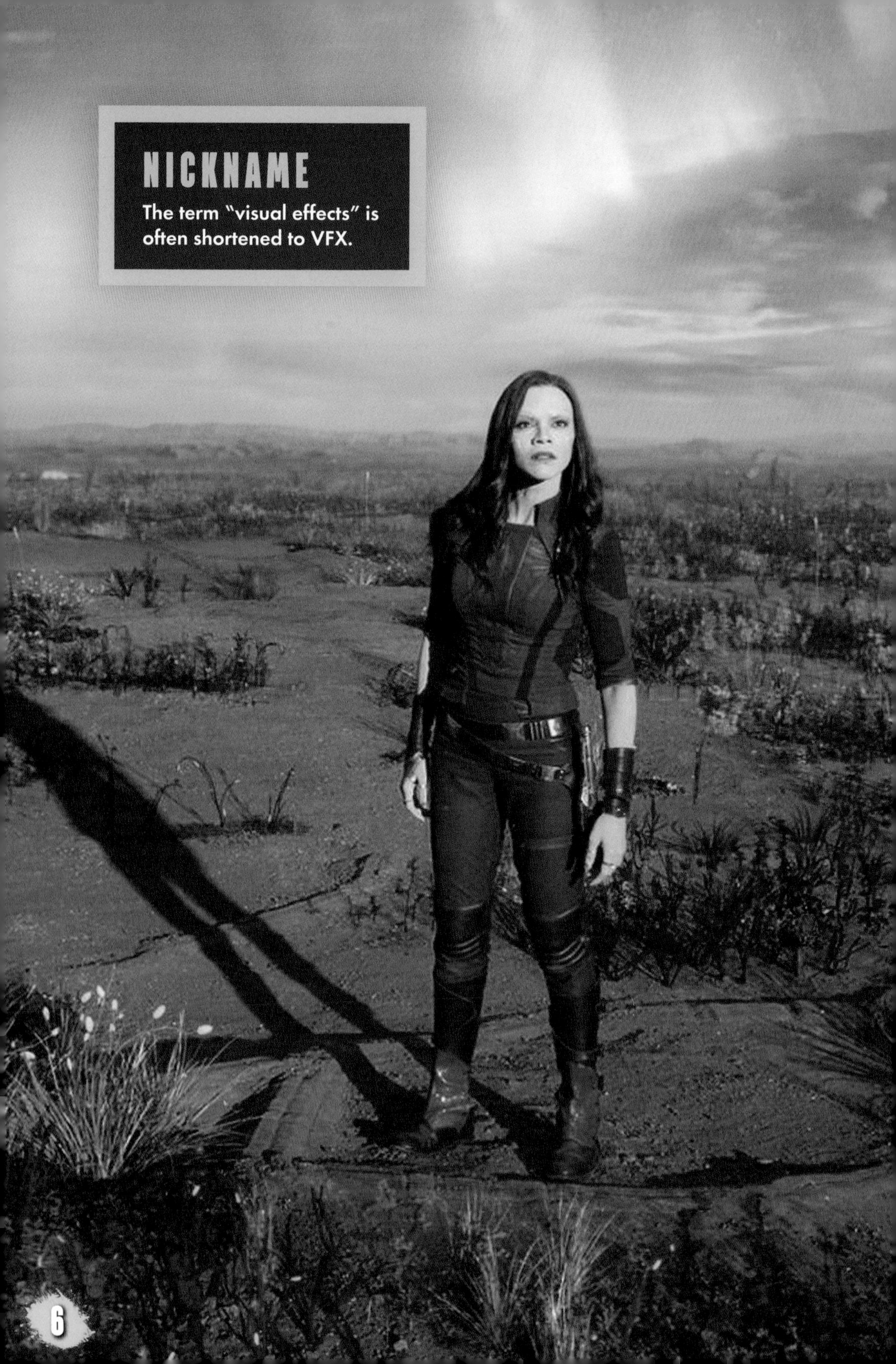

The film includes other computer-generated characters, too. Baby Groot looks like a tiny tree. The film begins with him dancing. The filmmakers used both CGI and motion capture to create this scene. Together, these effects made Baby Groot's dance moves look real.

Filmmakers also used visual effects to make some of the film's places. The planet Ego has unusual trees and waterfalls. Colorful bubbles float in the air. The entire planet is made up. CGI made it seem real!

ROCKET AND BABY GROOT

WHAT ARE VISUAL EFFECTS?

Visual effects are tricks filmmakers create during **post-production**. They are often combined with **practical effects** and **live-action** shots. Filmmakers use visual effects for scenes that would be impossible to **shoot** on set. Fictional things, such as monsters or alien worlds, become real on screen.

Visual effects also make it easier to film difficult or dangerous scenes. For example, filming from great heights is tricky. Filmmakers can use visual effects to create the views instead!

POST-PRODUCTION

THE WALK

SET EXTENSION FOR
JOHN CARTER

Visual effects are made in many ways. CGI is common. Artists create 3D images using computer software. These are added to films during post-production. On screen, the images look real!

A visual effect called set extension saves time and money. Some sets, like castles, are difficult to build. A construction team builds the part of the set where the actors perform. A visual effects team creates the rest of the building or landscape with CGI!

CGI JUNGLE

Wild animals in live-action films are often CGI. Examples include the monkeys in *Jumanji* and the tiger in *Life of Pi*.

Compositing is another important visual effect. Artists combine separate images into one image for a scene. For example, live-action scenes are often shot in front of a **green screen**. They are filmed multiple times. Then the shots are combined using a computer.

Compositors can also add snow, rain, fog, or any other thing that was not on set during shooting. They can also remove things, such as wires, stains, or reflections that do not belong in a scene.

ON THE SET OF
JUSTICE LEAGUE

N78298

NO MATCHING COLORS!

Colors that match the green screen will disappear. Actors who wear green clothes in front of a green screen will appear to have a floating head!

HISTORY OF VISUAL EFFECTS

In the early days of film, computer-generated visual effects were not possible. Instead, filmmakers used practical effects. **Miniatures** and **matte paintings** were often used to create new places. Early movies such as 1933's *King Kong* used matte paintings to create jungle scenes!

Practical effects were also often created with cameras. One popular camera trick was the **double exposure**. It made ghosts look real!

MATTE WORK

The 1954 film *20,000 Leagues Under the Sea* used matte paintings to create a stunning undersea world. The effects were also used to create a mysterious island called Vulcania.

MINIATURES IN *KING KONG*

STAR WARS: EPISODE IV –
A NEW HOPE

The 1970s saw the introduction of digital visual effects. The 1973 film *Westworld* was the first to use 2D computer graphics. Two minutes of computer-generated pixilation were used to show vision through a robot's eyes. Three years later, *Futureworld* was the first to use 3D computer graphics!

The 1977 blockbuster hit *Star Wars: Episode IV – A New Hope* broke new ground in visual effects. The filmmakers invented new ways to use cameras, computers, and miniatures to create epic space battles!

VISUAL EFFECTS PIONEERS

Names: John Whitney Jr. and George Demos
Known For: Computer animation artists who created the first computer graphics used in movies in *Westworld* (1973) and *Futureworld* (1976)
Awards: *Westworld* nominated for several best movie lists by American Film Institute

Visual effects skyrocketed during the 1980s. Many CGI firsts happened during this period.

Tron, released in 1982, had more CGI footage than any film ever before. Two years later, *The Last Starfighter* was released. It was the first film to feature spaceships and planets made with CGI instead of miniatures. The 1985 movie *Young Sherlock Holmes* featured the first completely CGI character to appear on the big screen. The character was a fearsome knight made from stained glass!

FLYING BIKES

The 1982 film *E.T. The Extra-Terrestrial* featured a visual effect with flying bikes. Cranes lifted and lowered the bikes in front of a blue screen. Artists later combined this footage with live-action scenes. This made the bikes appear to fly!

TRON

19

More CGI firsts were to come. The 1989 film *Indiana Jones and the Last Crusade* was the first movie to contain all-digital compositing. Filmmakers used it to make a character shrivel to ash!

The 1989 film *The Abyss* was the first to use CGI to make water effects. Artists created a 3D alien that shimmered and flowed just like seawater!

A WATERY PROJECT

It took a film crew for *The Abyss* about six months to make a scene featuring an alien made of water. On screen, the scene lasts only 75 seconds.

INDIANA JONES
AND THE LAST CRUSADE

FORREST GUMP

Visual effects continued expanding through the 1990s. Filmmakers began mixing CGI and live-action in ways never seen before. In 1993, *Jurassic Park* was the first film to feature realistic CGI animals.

A year later, *Forrest Gump* used CGI in a fun way. Artists used compositing to insert past presidents and other historic figures into scenes. The characters appeared to be talking directly to Forrest!

A FRIENDLY GHOST

The ghost Casper in the 1995 film *Casper* was the first CGI lead character in a full-length live-action film.

BLOCKBUSTER VISUALS

Today, more movies than ever are made with CGI. CGI and motion capture brought Gollum to life in the Lord of the Rings film series. CGI was also behind many characters in the Harry Potter films. They included the house elves, dementors, and the Hungarian horntail dragon.

The 2007 film *The Golden Compass* had nearly 1,200 CGI images. The talking animals, the Arctic landscape, and the magical dust looked real. But they all were made on computers!

A CURIOUS EFFECT
Benjamin's head is completely CGI for the first 52 minutes of the 2008 film *The Curious Case of Benjamin Button*.

THE GOLDEN COMPASS

25

WAKANDA IN
BLACK PANTHER

Superhero films also have a lot of visual effects. For example, characters often fly or leap from tall buildings. The actors are attached to wires and cables to shoot these scenes. Later, artists use computers to erase this equipment.

Many stunning places in superhero films are also made with CGI. The city of Atlanta, Georgia, became Wakanda for the 2018 film *Black Panther*. The made-up world of Atlantis sparkles with CGI colors in the 2018 film *Aquaman*!

NOTABLE VISUAL EFFECT

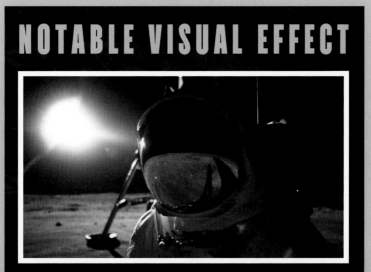

Movie: *First Man*
Year: 2018
Director: Damien Chazelle
Visual Effect: Scenes from space were created using CGI combined with live-action footage from the real 1969 moon landing

MOVING FORWARD

Visual effects continue to improve as technology advances. For example, artists struggle to make CGI humans look real. Their facial expressions often seem odd. Motion capture advances should solve this problem. CGI humans could soon look and move like human actors!

Camera systems are also changing. Future filmmakers may not need blue or green screens to create fictional locations. Instead, new camera systems will place actors directly into CGI locations during a shoot. Film possibilities are endless with visual effects!

FAN FAVORITES

Many popular animated movies of the past are being remade into CGI films. Examples include the 2019 films *Dumbo* and *The Lion King*!

AVATAR

MODERN VISUAL EFFECTS MASTER

Name: James Cameron
Born: August 16, 1954,
in Ontario, Canada
Known For: Filmmaker famous for
blockbuster films such as *Avatar* (2009),
in which visual effects techniques like
3D cameras and motion capture created an alien world
Awards: Many awards, including three Academy Awards each
for *Titanic* (1997) and *Avatar*

GLOSSARY

2D—showing only length and height

3D—showing length, height, and depth

CGI—artwork created by computers; CGI stands for computer-generated imagery.

compositing—a visual effect in which artists combine separate images into one image for a scene

digital—related to electronic or computer technology

double exposure—a piece of film that is exposed twice; a double exposure shows one image on top of another image.

footage—filmed material made for movies or television

green screen—a green backdrop upon which images are added after filming is completed; green screens are used interchangeably with blue screens.

live-action—filmed using real actors

matte paintings—fake sets made with paint

miniatures—small models

motion capture—a technology that matches human movement to computer-generated characters

pixilation—a technique in which the movements of real people are made to appear like animations

post-production—the period after filming during which visual effects are added

practical effects—special effects done on set during filming

scene—the action in a single place and time in a film or play

set—the place where a movie is made

set extension—a visual effects technique in which a landscape, building, or other part of a set created with CGI

shoot—the act of filming a movie

software—computer programs that do specific tasks

TO LEARN MORE

AT THE LIBRARY

Green, Sara. *Special Effects*. Minneapolis, Minn.:
Bellwether Media, 2019.

Hammelef, Danielle S. *Eye-Popping CGI:
Computer-Generated Special Effects*. North Mankato,
Minn.: Capstone Press, 2015.

Owen, Ruth. *Creating Visual Effects for Movies as a
CGI Artist*. New York, N.Y.: Bearport Publishing, 2016.

ON THE WEB

FACTSURFER

Factsurfer.com gives you
a safe, fun way to find
more information.

1. Go to www.factsurfer.com.

2. Enter "visual effects" into the search box
   and click 🔍.

3. Select your book cover to see a list
   of related web sites.

INDEX